UNDERSTANDING
Spiritual Warfare

Satan as a Roaring Lion

Frank N. Mitchell

This UNDERSTANDING booklet is part of a series of booklets on key issues of our time on the Reign of Christ at
www.ashiningcityonahill.org
www.reignofchrist.org
All booklets are available at amazon.com

September 2018

Preface

This UNDERSTANDING booklet is one in a series of booklets concerning **THE REIGN OF CHRIST** for our time and how that Reign plays out in all history and as foretold in the Bible.

The problem that I have encountered over the last 30 or 40 years is that Christians who think we should be praying and working for the Kingdom to come on Earth (in order to have the thousand year Reign of Christ in all its fullness) are generally Liberals and apostates who have a false and counterfeit Social Gospel and Social Justice message and understanding of the Kingdom come on Earth and of any possible millennial era of Christ.

On the other hand solid Bible-believing Christians, for a variety of reasons, often tend to be what are called amillennialists and premillennialists, and these folks generally think we are *not* to be praying or working for the Kingdom outside of some minor evangelism and works of charity. Their view is, tragically, that Jesus told us to hunker down in the churches and to wait for Him to return and for this current age to end or the world to end as we know it.

The practical importance of all of this cannot be overstated. It means few if any conservative Bible commentators are really thinking about what it would mean for the Kingdom of God to come on

Earth in all its fullness in the much prophesied worldwide Reign of Christ.

And to further complicate these matters there are many aspects to an actual Kingdom Era come here on planet Earth, and there are many obstacles to how such a Kingdom might well play out in actual history. And, finally, for a true Kingdom come on Earth there are many interrelated political, religious and economic difficulties and confusions in our time to be resolved and overcome.

Given this situation, each booklet in this UNDERSTANDING series tends to stand on its own in order to address some given specific problem or set of problems concerning a coming millennial era on Earth where we will see the nations or "kingdoms of this world become the kingdoms of our Lord and of His Christ."

In this coming time, *each shall know the Lord from the least to the greatest* and *the knowledge of God will fill the whole world as waters cover the sea*. And in this Kingdom time, we will see, worldwide, true worship of God in Spirit and Truth, and we will see all the nations in harmonious interaction in Peace, Justice, and Righteousness.

This will then be the much prophesied and long anticipated reign of the Son of David in a worldwide Reign of Christ.

Frank Mitchell

UNDERSTANDING
Spiritual Warfare
Satan as a Roaring Lion

First Peter 5:8b says, "...your adversary the devil, as a roaring lion, walks about, seeking whom he may devour." The question is do Satan's devils *really* do this or do they really not do this? The answer is they really do, but this is imagery. Satan is *like* or *as* a roaring lion. Satan is not going to physically eat, say, one's arm, and further, it isn't Satan doing the eating. There is only one lead demon, and that is Satan, but Satan is not as God who is ever-present.

Satan is limited to a specific time and place. Most ordinary people just get a junior demon to devour them, as C. S. Lewis correctly says in *The Screwtape Letters*. The problem is that modern man generally does not believe in demons, and tragically, modern man since the atheist-humanist Enlightenment often does not believe in God at all, and if he does, it will not be the God of Scripture but usually of Gnostic Liberalism or mystical Unitarianism, etc.

One might say that all of the atheists as well as all false-God folks have, quite tragically, already been devoured; they just do not know it! They mistakenly think they have figured out there is no actual God of Scripture who created the universe and everything in it. Such thinking, as Thomas Jefferson said, is a self-evident absurdity to the non-devoured. Having said this, Christian believers in my experience generally speaking do not have a proper understanding of demons or the topic of demons. About five or six years ago I decided to do a systematic study of the topic of demons starting with *The Screwtape Letters*, and I was quite surprised by what I found out, but I always did my study of various treatments of the topic against the backdrop of Scripture.

Demons 101
The first thing I found out in my study was that I had what might be called a standard interpretation of demons that I thought was consistent with Scripture, but it was not, as I was to find out. Indeed, my common misunderstanding of demons was one of the main reasons Lewis wrote *The Screwtape Letters*, he said himself, that is, to correct people's common misunderstandings of demons and how they can and often do work in our lives. A common problem is that in the Bible Jesus will cast demons out of people who have lost all control of themselves and cannot be restrained or are throwing themselves into fires and similar things. There is a tendency I have found to think that if one does not have such problems, one has no problems with demons and cannot be demon possessed or demon plagued, but the Bible clearly does not teach this.

So, how does a devil devour one? By giving one really stupid or foolish ideas or irrational ideas that are un-Godly ideas or temptations to sin or to be disrespectful or hateful to others or not faithful to God, etc., and one acts upon those ideas to one's detriment and gets "devoured." Indeed, this is what *The Screwtape Letters* is about. That book is about devils putting such destructive ideas into a new Christian believer's head. In my opinion, these are probably thoughts that Lewis himself actually had, and Lewis decided at some point those thoughts or ideas were actually literally of demons. If one gives one's self over to such demonic thoughts, one then makes a "shipwreck" of one's life, faith or ministry, says Paul, and when this happens, one has been ensnared by a demon with foolish teachings, actions, and ideas, etc. (See 1 Timothy 1 and 2 Timothy 2.)

Paul also says, famously, do not let the sun go down on one's anger lest one give place (quite literally) to the devil (Ephesians 4:26-27), and from this it would seem a root of bitterness can (quite literally) take hold in one's life (Hebrews 12:15). We do not understand exactly how any of this works, but we do understand that it happens. There are literal spiritual adversaries to us as humans who want to keep us from God in Christian salvation and who want to mess up our lives and/or ministries after we come to Christ. Satan (that is, one of his demons) is trying to get you over to sin, abusing others, and opposing God, etc. This takes one into his spiritual camp, and it can and often will eventually lead to eternal damnation with him or to making a shipwreck of one's salvation and Christian life.

Deliverance Ministries

A key problem here is that in many churches demons and the problems of demons are never discussed, and there is a common view that Christians cannot be demon possessed, based on the view that Christians have the Holy Spirit in them and He will not let demons come into a believer. I know of no Scripture passage that says that, and it seems inconsistent with almost all other passages on the topic, and further over many years Frank and Ida Hammond (as recorded in the book *Pigs in the Parlor*) cast demons out of hundreds of Christians in their deliverance ministry. Further, they would not bother to cast a demon out of non-Christians because the demon can go right back into that person. That is to say, if one has a demonic spirit that is plaguing one and that has taken root in one's soul or psyche, in order to get deliverance from that demon spirit, one needs to be saved or born again and one needs to want the deliverance in the name of Jesus.

In truth, if one is consumed (if not strictly "possessed") by a **spirit of resentment** about something, even if quite justified, it can ruin one's relationships and life more generally, and demon or no demon, one can want deliverance from it by the power of the Spirit of God in Christ. But, one must ask, is that spirit of resentment *necessarily* a literal demon? I would say not necessarily but quite possibly, according to Scripture. For example, I knew of a homosexual once who said he had tried to "pray gay away," and after he prayed, he still had homosexual urges so he decided to return to his gay lifestyle. Tragically, to his eternal destruction, this guy did not understand in at least three or four ways what the Bible has to say on these sorts of matters.

For deliverance, he has to first get saved, that is, denounce his homosexuality and its practice and commit to follow Jesus, while trusting in the atoning sacrifice of Christ for his salvation. This he did not do. Second, even if he had taken this first crucial step, which he did not by his own statement, the Bible does not say he will not still be tempted to sin (in homosexuality or otherwise) after he gets saved. Rather, the Bible says God's Spirit in us helps give us the victory over sin. Third, one's homosexuality might not be a demon, but it might be, but either way God can ultimately deliver one from its controlling power even if there is a struggle there.

What the Hammonds found in their many years of deliverance ministry is that they had amazing success casting such demons out of people, *if* those people had committed to Christ and *if* they truly wanted deliverance. The Hammonds would not send the demons to the bottomless pit because they felt Scripture does not allow for that until the end of the age. However, in this writer's opinion, this is clearly the end of the age, and this would mean any and all demons should be consigned to the pit in any such deliverance ministry today.

In a similar way, the same sort of thing is at play more overtly with transsexuals today. The transsexual not only has the urge to become a member of the opposite sex, but actually feels there is an actual spirit living inside of them that is of the opposite sex and it has its own name and identity. For example, Sam has an overwhelming feeling that there is a real "Sally" living inside of him that he wants to become, and so he wants to have a sex change operation. Is this a demon? Presumably, but again perhaps not, but it is not exactly a sexual thing, any more than it would be if a person was convinced that Napoleon Bonaparte was literally inside of him. What's the point? The transsexual is not seeking deliverance from a spirit he feels is inside of him, in fact, just the opposite. He is giving in to the spirit that he is convinced is in him. And, again, this is the case whether one is a Christian or not, but again, it is only in Christ that one can potentially get control of the situation and will have spiritual authority over any possible demonic spirit in order to cast it out and send it to the bottomless pit. However such deliverance can be a bit complicated.

Though they can never really be confirmed, the stories tend to be very similar. A very brave GI or successful male athlete, who is often a Christian, struggles secretly, literally for decades, with a female spirit living inside him, until finally after much counseling, Christian and otherwise, he decides to take the plunge and have a sex-change operation.

And he is then written up in various tabloids where he does a tell-all story of the whole thing, etc.

However, invariably in such stories the transsexual **never** went to a deliverance ministry over the many years of his struggle in order to get demon deliverance, if that in fact was what was needed, which it would seem it was. Further, as he struggled over the decades with his indwelling female spirit, he usually says he would wear women's underwear under his male clothing. This was a big mistake because so long as he was wearing women's underwear, the demon spirit had **a right** to possess him or to be in him, etc. In deliverance ministries, as is well-known, one must get rid of anything that gives a demon a right to come into one's life.

If one is an idol worshipper, one must get rid of all one's idols and demonic charms and certainly stop wearing them and so forth, or one is not in a position to allow the authority of Jesus to work over demons in the realm of the spirit. There is set dynamic here. Get saved for sure, take off and throw out demonic charms, women's clothing, etc., and then cast out the demon and send it to the bottomless pit. The transsexual GI or athlete, etc., often does just the opposite after making sure of his love for Christ.

Such a guy in these cases was probably not demon-possessed initially, but Satan was going about like a roaring lion seeking to devour him, and demon spirits can plague such men with a bizarre (in fact, demonic and un-Godly) urge, literally for years these guys will say, to wear a bra, a dress or panties or whatever. And once a guy gives in to that urge and goes out and buys his very own women's underwear and then begins to wear it full-time under his male clothes, the transsexual demon has an actual right to come into the man, but not until then.

Once one, in effect, invites a female demon spirit into one's life by constantly wearing women's underwear for years, no less, and that spirit then takes root, it is not going to leave of its own volition. That is for sure. (If one reads the literature, this is the testimony of countless transsexuals who have no idea what has hit them or why.)

Spiritual Authority in Christ
The larger point here is that there is a spiritual dynamic of authority at work in the power of Christ over demonic forces because of the atoning work of Christ on the Cross, where Christ took back the title deed to planet Earth and was given "all authority" on Earth. (See Matthew 28:18)

After Pentecost there will be a spreading of Christ's Kingdom and spiritual authority over demons throughout the Church Age until Christians in Christ push back the powers of evil, darkness, and deception completely. Scripture in numerous places seems pretty clear that finally the whole planet will be secured in the realm of the spirit for Christ and his Kingdom and that the demonic forces will be bound or kicked out of the whole world and consigned to the bottomless pit for the next thousand years. (See Revelation 20:1-3)

Before this happens Satan and his demonic hordes will fight back by energizing the lost world to attack and persecute Christians, and really for little or no reason, if you stop and think about it except for the fact they are Christians. As early Christians argued as they were persecuted in the Roman Empire, Christians are actually good for a nation because they tend to make such good law-abiding citizens! This means persecutions of Christians and attacks upon Christians are generally irrational and usually make no sense unless one sees them as demonically inspired.

This was true in the Roman Empire, and it has been true throughout history. And the same is true today of the horrible persecutions of Christians in Muslim countries with their pagan spirituality of the unholy Koran and their false god Allah and his false prophet Mohammad, who gives new meaning to the modern notion of true hate speech!

The fact is when the Gospel is openly and correctly preached, people tend to come to Jesus by the thousands, and Satan knows that and so he has to kill or imprison Christians to silence them in order to stop the spread of Christ's Kingdom throughout the whole world. But besides working in direct opposition to the Church **outside** the Church, demons somehow work *inside* the Church as something of a fifth column to corrupt its message with "doctrines of devils" and to cause strife, division, contention, one-upsmanship, and arguing about unimportant matters. Doctrines of demons virtually summon demons into one's life and fellowship. In the Church these doctrines are usually not outright evils that can be easily recognized but rather deceptive false goods.

Doctrines of Demons: Social Justice and Sectarianism

There are countless warnings in Scripture about doctrines of devils and wolves in sheep's clothing and so forth, and this is another way Satan, as a roaring lion, devours fellowships and the lives of Christians. *If* one sees the falseness of a teaching, it is easy to see, but *if* one does not see the falseness of a teaching, then it is not easy to see. Doctrines of demons are generally irrational, confused, immoral, ungodly, and so forth, but if one is deceived by them one thinks one is getting new unprecedented higher insights, etc.

For example, C. S. Lewis says demons put such false teachings in the head of pastors to preach as true and good, thus literally invoking demons into a worship service! A classic demonic false teaching for our time (says Lewis) is that Social Justice is a good, and not an evil. And from there Lewis says demons convince pastors and Christian teachers to take the next step that Social Justice is the point of the Christian faith!!!

Once one sees how this works, it tends to become quite obvious and fairly easy to deal with, and one is as Paul says in one translation "exposing" the works of darkness. (Ephesians 5:11) For example, **Social Justice** is Socialist or Communist "Justice," which is the state redistributing wealth to make us all equal. Social Justice, where one does not get to keep the fruits of one's own labor, is meant as the opposite of classical Justice. Countless essays have been written on this, but regardless there are Social Justice movements within many churches that people, pastors, and teachers get on board for as supposedly true and brilliant. In my experience, rarely are pastors and teachers in such churches aware of the well-known evils of Social Justice.

At the initial point Social Justice ideas can be *only* in one's head, so to speak, as false facts and false goods, but if one takes Social Justice teachings to heart as the point of the faith, then it goes from head to heart in a literal spiritual sense, and one becomes a so-called "Social Justice Warrior." One is then energized, motivated, driven, etc., to work for Social Justice and to vote for Social Justice candidates and to give them money and so forth and so on, all the while thinking one is doing the Lord's work as one is on fire for and possessed (literally or figuratively) by a spirit of the devil's false and evil Social Justice as a good. This particular demonic deception and spiritual reality is probably the rule rather the exception in many if not most mainline churches today. Obviously, many well-meaning Christian people, teachers, and preachers have not read their Lewis or their Paul or their Peter too carefully!

Excessive denominationalism or excessive sectarianism is also demonic. How do we know this? Accepting the truth of any given denomination is not the point of the faith, and most denominations have at least some flaws and certainly some deficiencies to the Whole Counsel of the Kingdom of God. In fact, simply accepting even the truth of the Bible itself is not the point of the faith, as James tells us, famously no less, but a lot of people have not read their James either.

The Two Great Commandments
The point of the Christian faith, indeed the very point of life is twofold: one, are you saved, and two, are you saved unto good works? The devil wants one preaching anything but this no matter how good or true, let alone how false and deceptive. And this twofold central point of the Christian faith is all through Scripture. And it is summed up in the Two Great Commandments of love God with all your heart, mind, and soul, and love your neighbor as yourself. Are you right with God and in loving fellowship with Him, and are you living right with others, or are you not? This is the message of Scripture over and over and over again. For example, Matthew 6:33 says, "Seek ye first the Kingdom of

God (in the Holy Spirit) and God's (or the Kingdom's) Righteousness (of good works) and these other things (of life shall) be added to you." Or 1 Peter 2:24 says, "[Christ] Himself bore our sines in His own body on the tree, that we, having died to sins might live for righteousness."

For the Two Great Commandments the Devil substitutes his Two Great Falsehoods, namely, the universal fatherhood of God and the universal brotherhood of man. This is commonplace in the Liberal and apostate churches, and there it is the rule rather than the exception. Indeed, the Two Great Falsehoods tend to be the identifying mark of Christian Liberalism says the great Christian scholar J. Gresham Machen. To this the Devil adds the idea that Christ died on the Cross not to reconcile us to God (which is the clear teaching of Scripture) but to reconcile us to each other or merely to end tribalism or to establish the universal brotherhood of mankind, etc.

However, some churches do **not** substitute the Two Great Falsehoods of Liberalism for the Two Great Commandments or substitute the false atoning work of Christ for the true atoning work, but rather they **add** them to the Two Great Commandments and true atoning work, in an effort to complete the faith, as it were.

Adding the Two Great Falsehoods to the Christian faith is **also** a clear demonic confusion and deception because the Two Great Falsehoods actually negate the Two Great Commandments. And "No man can serve two (opposing) masters," as Christ said, "for either he will hate the one, and love the other; or else he will hold to the one, and despise the other." (Matthew 6:24) Or as Paul said, "What fellowship hath righteousness with unrighteousness? and what communion hath light with darkness? And what concord hath Christ with Belial (the Devil)?" (2 Corinthians 6:14-15) No fellowship, obviously, and if anyone tries to pull off this mixture, he is going to get, and indeed is being, devoured. However, in the demonic deception of serving two masters or mixing Christ worship with Satan worship, one foolishly thinks one is fixing, improving or completing the Christian faith. The same is true with the so-called "Social Gospel."

Doctrines of Demons: The Social Gospel
The Liberal's Social Gospel says that the point of the faith and of the Gospel is doing selfless works of charity. Is that true? No, that is not true. Selfless works of charity can be fine things in appropriate circumstances, but that is not the Gospel, which is Christ died on the Cross for our sins to reconcile us to God and to give us new spiritual life in Him. Further, selfless works of charity are not only not the Gospel, they are not the general point of the Christian faith in dealing with others. The Golden Rule is, which is "Do unto others as you would have them do unto you," or that is to say, yet again, the

Second Great Commandment of "Love your neighbor as yourself."

The Golden Rule or Second Great Commandment is the point of our interaction with others. This may indeed at times include selfless works of charity, but such works are not the general point of the faith, which is the moral virtue of the Golden Rule or the Second Great Commandment, as both Jesus said in Matthew (22:34-40) and Paul in Romans (13:9). And, further, the "selfless works of charity" standard of the Liberal is not only not moral virtue, as such, nor the general point of the Christian faith, as such, it is utopian as a general standard. So, as a false-good general standard of the Devil, selfless works of charity is neither moral nor practical, both of which God's Word **always** is, as is common sense, no less.

Further, the false teaching of Satan holds to "the universal fatherhood of God," which says all religions worship the same God but by a different name. That is clearly a false teaching and a demonic absurdity. This false teaching and view of Christian Liberalism is the centerpiece of the end-time one-world religion of Satan himself, and anyone who practices this demonic religion with its demonic spirituality has been devoured, tragically. At the same time, "the universal brotherhood of man" is not just a false morality for the Second Great Commandment or Golden Rule, it is no morality at all!

The whole point of "the universal brotherhood of man" is to say there is *no* salvation in Christ to create the saved as opposed to the lost or to create a need for salvation. The whole point of Christian salvation is that we become brothers and sisters **in Christ** in the realm of the spirit as born-again children in a way we were not before. The entire point of the Liberal's demonic "universal brotherhood of man" is this is not the case!

The Hammonds, interestingly, cast demons of false doctrinal positions out of people. However, Paul's instruction in dealing with these sorts of demonic false-teaching and false-doctrine problems is a bit different. He says avoid "foolish and ignorant questionings... knowing that they gender strifes. And the Lord's servant must not strive, but be gentle towards all, apt to teach, forbearing, in meekness correcting them that oppose themselves; if perhaps God may give them repentance unto the knowledge of the truth, that they may recover themselves out of the snare of the devil, having been taken captive by him unto his will." (2 Timothy 2:23-25)

We can in our errors have a moment of enlightenment: "Good grief! I can see it! How could I have been so foolish!" The fact is demonic deception and ensnarement can be as obvious as the nose on your face when you come to see it but not until then if one has been "ensnared" (as Paul says) by demonic deception.

The Devil works in two ways. He works in outright evil such as hate and conflict, and he works in deceptive false goods such as agape love as lawlessness, which is central tenet of ancient Gnosticism as well as modern Liberalism. The similar false notion of "unconditional love" is a false (and demonic) concept of agape love (of unconditional acceptance) that came out of atheist humanism in the 1930s, specifically for the purpose of displacing classical concepts of agape love found in the Bible, common sense, and Western civilization.

Believing in false goods and thinking they are brilliant and truly good is a false enlightenment, and when one takes them to heart and acts upon them, one has been devoured. Here we have seen some of the more common demonic errors and deceptions of our time. Social Justice is the Devil's false Justice. The Social Gospel is the Devil's false Gospel. Unconditional love is the Devil's false love. And the universal brotherhood of man is the Devil's false moral standard, and the universal fatherhood of God is the Devil's false religion.

Indeed, the universal fatherhood of God is the false end-time religion of the Whore of Babylon in Revelation and of the end-time apostate Church of Laodicea with a different Jesus and different Gospel. Once all of these things are seen clearly for what they are Satan is finished, presumably.

Conclusion

There are many ways to be devoured by a demon to sin or to do outright evil or foolishness or to do false goods that in the end lead only to heartache and destruction, for the devil comes only to kill, rob, and destroy, as Jesus told us. (John 10:10) Christians are in no way exempt from this. This does not mean that one loses one's salvation, but one can make a shipwreck of one's life, ministry or service to God with no treasures laid up in heaven because all one's supposed good works can be no more than wood, hay, and stubble and not gold, silver, and precious stones. (1 Corinthians 3:12)

So, the real larger question is, "Are you truly saved? Are you truly in Christ in order to have the abundant spiritual life of John 10:10?" because a demonic deception here on this issue has eternal consequences for every human being on planet Earth and because, as someone said many, many years ago, the road to hell is paved with good but foolish intentions and demonic deceptions for those truly devoured by Satan. Oh, the eternal tragedy of it all!

On the other hand, when people see the glorious light of the Gospel clearly, not blinded by Satan, they will in this writer's experience almost invariably open their hearts to Christ to come in and have fellowship with Him with a peace that passes all understanding. It is a wonderful thing, indeed.

In the Lord's Prayer we pray to be delivered from the Evil One so "the Kingdom can come on earth as it is heaven." This means the Lord's Prayer is, in effect, a binding and loosing prayer in the heavenly realm. And Scripture teaches in Revelation 20 that after the saints in Christ and Christ in the saints have defeated the final great demonic deceptions and evils of one-world government and one-world religion that then the angels are going to bind Satan in the bottomless pit and presumably then or with time all of his demonic hordes as well, and at that time the Lord's Prayer asking for the Kingdom to "come on earth as in heaven," a prayer which has been prayed countless millions of times, will be answered in all its fullness.

===

Other booklets on the Reign of Christ in this UNDERSTANDING Series:

UNDERSTANDING Prophecy Fulfillment:
The Great Apostasy, Babylon, Mystery Babylon & the Reign of Christ

This little booklet gives an overview of the central major prophecies concerning the possible soon coming Reign of Christ. Specifically these are the prophecies of the Great Apostasy, Babylon, Mystery Babylon, and the man of lawlessness. These prophecies are seen as fulfilled in the false millennial visions of Marx and of the New World Order of UN Agenda 21 and Agenda 2030 and in the Liberal World Council of Churches.

UNDERSTANDING All Bible Prophecy:
Genesis to Revelation

This booklet holds that all prophecy should be interpreted in terms of the larger story of the Bible and the larger story of the Christian cosmology from the Creation to the Final Judgment, and this is especially the case for the book of Revelation.

UNDERSTANDING Globalism:
What is the "New World Order"?

This booklet looks at what "globalism" is generally and at the related topic of a "New World Order" that actually has **very** specific definitions and formulations that are often not well-known.

UNDERSTANDING Revelation 19:
Victory over One-World Government and One-World Religion

Revelation 19 though very controversial is actually very straightforward. The saints in a Marriage Supper of the Lamb move into a new more mature, intimate, and complete relationship with Christ, and then the saints in Christ and Christ in the saints completely and totally defeat the evils of one-world government and one-world religion. Simple enough when you get right down to it.

UNDERSTANDING Statesmanship
Classical Justice *versus* Social Justice

Probably no two notions are more misunderstood as well as more necessary to understand in our time than classical Justice and Social Justice. This booklet looks at the history of these two terms and how one stands for the Justice of statesmanship for doing the common good and the other for the injustice of special interest groups and wealth redistribution as a false human right for economic equality.

UNDERSTANDING Alternative Political Universes:
The Natural Revelation & Self-Evident Truths

For some folks as Jefferson and the American founders, the Natural Law or so-called Higher Moral Law is a self-evident truth, but for others with a reprobate mind and no common sense, this is not the case at all. These modern-day people who have lost their common sense are just as the ancient Epicureans (atheist hedonists) while modern-day Liberals are just as ancient Gnostics with their false enlightenment and false morality. Understand these things, and you will pretty well understand Alternative Political Universes.

UNDERSTANDING Illegal Immigration:
The Wall and All It Stands For

"The Wall" of Donald Trump stands for many larger issues from exposing hypocrisy among professional politicians to ending globalism, open borders, and the often total lawlessness of our time. Lawlessness of the Liberal and atheist-humanist is, in fact, the spirit of anti-Christ.

UNDERSTANDING The Whole Counsel of the Kingdom:
The Central Message of Jesus and Paul

Both Jesus and Paul preached a Whole Counsel of the Kingdom message, but this is not a generally well-known truth. This booklet looks at the concept of a Whole Counsel of the Kingdom Christianity and what it entails, namely, true worship of God in Spirit and Truth as well as Just and Righteous government.

UNDERSTANDING Spiritual Warfare:
Satan as a Roaring Lion

Scripture tells us that Satan goes about like a roaring lion seeking whom he may devour, but this is generally not a very understood warning, and tragically many people, if not devoured completely, get an arm or leg eaten (so to speak). To be forewarned is to be forearmed. This booklet deals with ways to recognize and deal with demons.

===

All of the above booklets are part of a series on key issues of our time on the Reign of Christ at
www.ashiningcityonahill.org
www.reignofchrist.org

All of the above booklets are put together in a single **Volume I** called

UNDERSTANDING The Reign of CHRIST
The One Big Issue of Our Time
Volume I

This Volume I of all the above booklets together as well as all of the above booklets separately are available at **amazon.com**